The DNA of the Autonomous Attorney

Free Webinar Revealing the 3 Keys to success: www.7FigureLawFirm.com

Copyright © 2012 by Automated Business Results, LLC

All rights reserved. No part of this book may be used or reproduced in any manner whatsoever without prior written consent of the author, except as provided by the United States of America copyright law.

Published by Automated Business Results, LLC, Gilbert, Arizona.

Printed in the United States of America.

ISBN: 13: 9781484093214

Additional copies are available at special quantity discounts for bulk purchases for sales promotions, premiums, fundraising, and educational use.

For more information, please contact: Automated Business Results, LLC. 3303 East Baseline Road, Ste. 107k, Gilbert, AZ 85234. (888) 375-2573

Contact the author directly at richard@YourBusinessAutomated.com

---

The Publisher and Author make no representations or warranties with respect to the accuracy or completeness of the contents of this work and specifically disclaim all warranties, including without limitation warranties of fitness for a particular purpose. No warranty may be created or extended by sales or promotional materials. The advice and strategies contained herein may not be suitable for every situation. This work is sold with the understanding that the publisher is not engaged in rendering legal, account or other professional services. If professional assistance is required, the services of a competent professional person should be sought. Neither the Publisher nor the Author shall be liable for damages arising here from. The fact that an organization or website is referred to in this work as a citation and/or potential source of further information does not mean the that Author or Publisher endorses the information the organization or website may provide or recommendations it may make. Further, readers should be aware that the internet websites listed in this work may have changed or disappeared between when this work was written and when it was read.

Contents

Introduction 5
Secret #1 Manage Your Cash Flow 9
    Here's What NOT to Do 10
    Understanding and Tracking Your Cash Flow IS Your Job 11
    How and Why to Set Up Your Accounts 12
    Scott David Stewart on Cash Flow 14
Secret #2 Manage Your Staff 15
    Condition Your Clients to Use the System 16
    Evaluate What's Working 18
    Keep Kicking the Ball 20
    Scott David Stewart on Management 20
Secret #3 Systematize Your Work Flow 22
    What is Work Flow Management? 23
    The "Secret Sauce" Example 24
    You Must Decide How to Run Your Business 26
Secret #4 Make Marketing Your Top Priority 27
    Why Marketing Matters 28
    Developing Your Unique Competitive Advantage (UCA) 28
    Understanding Your "Who" 30
    Message to Market Match 31
    The Secret Key of Marketing 32
    Scott David Stewart on Marketing 34

Secret #5 Consistently Generate New Leads 35
- Capturing Leads 36
- Multiplying and Tracking Your Sources of Leads 37
- All These Lead Sources and All This Tracking Sounds Complicated 39

Secret #6 Convert New Leads into Cash 41
- Track Your Results to Improve Your Results 44

Secret #7 Measure Your Success with Key Performance Indicators 46
- Systematizing Your KPI Report 47
- Evaluating Your Progress 48
- Scott David Stewart on KPIs 49

Bonus Secret - Automate Your Systems 51
- D Pew on Automating Your Practice 51

A Final Word from the Author 52

Introduction

When was the last time you worked a 38-hour workweek?

While you work late into the night (and sometimes on weekends, I'm guessing?), Phoenix Bankruptcy Attorney "D" Pew is home evenings AND weekends spending time with his family, just like a "normal" dad.

No, he's not sacrificing income to be with his family. "D's" business created $2.14 MILLION in gross sales last year.

Divorce attorney Scott David Stewart isn't even taking cases anymore. He manages attorneys he's hired to make sure they're handling their cases properly and then spends his afternoons playing golf.

Scott is not losing money either. His business was up 70% since we started working together.

Did you ever wonder who decided working 60 hours a week is a pre-requisite to becoming a "successful" attorney? Or why so many attorneys continue to adhere to it?

You might answer, "To get everything done! To make good money!"

But that isn't the reason...not the real reason, anyway.

The fact is that you *can* earn the respect and the income you deserve, while still enjoying a full life outside your office!

You just haven't figured out how to do it yet.

How do I know?

My name is Richard James and I spent 18 months as the Business Manager and Marketing Director in "D" Pew's bankruptcy firm, designing and implementing the systems responsible for his firm's meteoric rise in the Phoenix market and for his ability to live life on his own terms rather than being at the mercy of his clients and his business.

I can tell you with absolute certainty that working 60-hour weeks is not a pre-requisite to success!

My specialty is taking attorneys who are tired of the rat race and turning them into multi-million dollar practice owners who can take time off at will.

We accomplished these amazing results by building their business on a foundation of concrete rather than quick sand.

Our systems ensure that every prospect is followed up with until either they decided to Buy, Die or Unsubscribe.

With these systems we focus on turning No's into Yes's.

Every time a prospect says:

- No, I don't want an appointment
- No, I don't want to show to the appointment I booked
- No, I don't want to hire you after your initial consultation

Our systems will automate follow-up with that prospect via e-mail, direct mail, text messaging and yes, the good old fashion telephone.

Last year we generated over a million in revenue for Lawrence "D" Pew and Scott David Stewart from prospects who originally said NO!

These systems have proven to be so powerful, effective and in demand that I've recently begun offering them nationwide to attorneys like you.

I tell you this for three specific reasons:

#1 I know what I'm talking about.

Everything you read in this book is based on real, live application in a working law firm like yours. These systems have led and will continue to lead attorneys to economic freedom and most importantly freedom of time. I know because I've helped attorneys like you achieve exactly that.

#2 I don't want you to be frustrated or fall into despair.

It's very easy to look at the seven systems I'll be teaching and proclaim, "I could NEVER do that! It's too complicated." If, after reading this book, you want to learn more or actually want help implementing the systems we cover, you have options.

I've created a home study course called "DNA of the 7-Figure Law Firm." It goes into greater detail and outlines specific strategies and practices you can begin implementing in your practice right away.

If you're interested in having my team automate your practice by implementing a system based on the "DNA of Autonomous Attorney," that may also be an option. (I say "may" because these services are in limited supply and by application only.)

#3 I don't want angry readers demanding to know, "Why didn't you tell me sooner?"

If you have the slightest interest in either the home study course or the nationwide done-for-you marketing program, I'm letting you know right now that those options are available to you.

This is NOT a sales pitch!

I'm simply trying to keep you happy by letting you know that opportunities for you to implement everything is this book and are available to you right now.

All you need to do is ask.

To learn more about the "DNA of a 7-Figure Law Firm" course, visit us online at:

www.7figurelawfirm.com/DNA

To receive an information package detailing our extensive done-for-you services, visit us online at:

www.YourPracticeAutomated.com

Freedom is something that you as an attorney deserve. You fight for people's rights day in and day out. You have the *right* to stop working at a decent hour of the day.

I'm here to show you how.

Secret #1
Manage Your Cash Flow

If you want to become a wealthy attorney, your primary business goal is to MAKE MONEY. This can be accomplished by capturing more clients, billing more client hours, and collecting more cash.

In order to measure how well you're achieving this number one business goal, you MUST have a system to manage it. You must have a system in place that tells you how much money you're bringing in every day, every week, every month and every year.

And to do this, you need to keep track of more than just the amount you billed.

If you *really* want to become a wealthy attorney, you need to start focusing on the money you've *collected*.

Here's What NOT to Do

When I first started working with my client "D" Pew, he was tracking the success of his bankruptcy firm using an Excel spreadsheet and a Word document. He was putting in all the transactions by hand, setting up formulas to add, subtract, divide and so forth.

While he ended up with a usable statement for his firm, the time it took him to manage the spreadsheet and input all the data was absolutely ridiculous. I wanted to tell him to add a line to calculate how much money he was losing by spending his OWN TIME putting this thing together.

And you can imagine what happened when a week or two went by and he hadn't had the time to get all the data into the spreadsheet! He was left with piles of transactions to enter which led to longer nights at the office and a greater level of anxiety because he had to start choosing between serving a client and getting his books up to date. Or he had to choose between going home to be with his family or getting his records up to date.

Not only that, until he got the records up to date he was operating his business blindly because he really couldn't tell what his current state of affairs really was!

If you are tracking your accounts in a spreadsheet or by hand, if you are tracking your accounts yourself rather than hiring a bookkeeper to do it for you, I can tell you right now that you are losing money.

For every hour you're spending handling your own accounts, you are losing the equivalent of your hourly rate.

It's disappearing into thin air.

You are losing money that you will never recapture!

Stop spending your time on account management. Get a bookkeeper. Set up a system. Start operating your business like a business!

Understanding and Tracking Your Cash Flow IS Your Job

While I don't want you handling the nitty-gritty recording of every transaction, I do want you to be looking at your Cash Flow position more often that you're probably doing now.

Again, if you're like most attorneys, you may only see your financial statements when your accountant hands them to you at the end of the year for your stamp of approval. And even then, do you *really* look at the statements or do you just say, "Yep! Looks great!" and sign off on them, relying on your CPA's competence to assure you that everything is alright?

At the very least, you should be looking at your cash flow situation monthly. The statement you'll want your bookkeeper or QuickBooks system to generate is your Profit and Loss statement also known as the Income Statement.

The Income Statement looks at the actual cash brought into the firm, subtracts all the cash applied to expenses and gives you the difference. The difference is called your Net Income (AKA Profit) or your Net Loss. That's why it is also referred to as the Profit and Loss Statement.

You should be looking at this statement AT LEAST once a month. (We review ours weekly)

And you should have a system in place to generate this statement for you automatically...at the touch of a button.

How and Why to Set Up Your Accounts

You'll want to set up your accounts in a manner similar to the Income Statement. Your incoming cash flow streams are represented in the top half. Your expenses are listed in the bottom half. Your goal is to make the difference a positive number that grows larger and larger each month.

Beyond just knowing how much you're keeping, you must use this information to determine where your cash is being spent and whether those expenses are truly benefitting your firm or not.

For example, if your money is going toward marketing, how much business is *each* marketing expense generating? What is the return on investment of each marketing dollar in each category? How much are you spending to generate a lead? How much are you spending to get a client? What is the average client value for each client who hires your firm?

If you don't know the answers to these questions, you are left in the dark when it comes to decision making.

So when you set up what's called your Chart of Accounts, you need to drill down deep. You can't just list "Advertising and Marketing" as one line item and dump all your expenditures into that one bucket. You need to break your expenses down into very discrete categories:

- Advertising
- Radio
- Station #1
- Station #2
- Station #3
- Television
- Station #1 ad #1
- Station #1 ad #2
- Station #2 Ad #1
- Station #2 Ad #2

- Yellow Pages
- Pay Per Click
- SEO/Website
- Direct Mail Campaign #1
- Direct Mail Campaign #2

Cash Flow management is not just about tracking how wealthy you are becoming; it's about putting yourself and your firm in a better decision-making position.

Because better decision-making is what will make you a wealthy attorney.

Scott David Stewart on Cash Flow

Rich and I see eye to on Cash Flow as a system because we both know and understand the importance of analyzing your reports, analyzing a Profit and Loss statement, looking at your Balance Sheet and being able to project and plan. Only then can you continue to build the other systems that help run your law firm so that you can put some money aside for reserves and so you can take profits out of your business.

Secret #2
Manage Your Staff

The goal of management is to control your world by controlling the behavior of the people around you.

When your world goes out of control, when you are plagued by constant interruptions and demands for your attention, your business-building energy is sapped dry and you are left wishing that somehow you could find the time to really work on your business.

Until you establish systems and policies to control the people who are running...and sometimes *ruining*...your world, you won't recapture your energy and you won't find the time.

If you're like most of my clients, managing staff is one of the deepest, darkest areas of your business. This is especially true when it comes to hiring and training additional attorneys you add to your team.

It may feel like herding cats!

The big secret when it comes to management is to establish a system and then train your staff *and* your clients to follow the system.

Condition Your Clients to Use the System

Your staff needs to behave a certain way in order to ensure your firm's success. But, what about your clients?

I'm sure you can think of at least a handful of tasks you wish your clients would accomplish in a timely manner, things you wish they would do and things you wish they wouldn't do. So why not condition them to get things done right from the start?

Here are a few examples of what we do at Pew Law Center...

First of all, we train clients that if they have a question they are to send it via email. We don't encourage them to call the firm when they want an update. We train them to communicate via email and then we track the emails and response time to answer each email. (We can track to the minute how long it takes us to get back to a client question)

When an email comes in it receives a time stamp and gets assigned to someone for their response. The system tracks how long it takes each email to be answered and generates a report on the average response time along with the total time spent by our staff answering emails.

Right now we're running at 11.5 hours to respond.

This keeps our clients *very* happy. They can be trained to communicate via email because we reward them with a timely response.

Another example is getting clients to show up for their court dates. We've created an automated reminder system that sends them a text, an email, and a live phone call reminder about their appointment.

In addition, because the courthouse in Phoenix is hard to find, we send an email with a video that shows them exactly how to get there. We actually have "D" Pew narrating the directions so that clients can actually see the road they will be traveling and where they need to turn to find parking. They receive all this information before even leaving their house. This helps decrease the client's anxiety prior to arriving at the hearing.

We repeat the process for their initial appointment to our office. We automate the delivery of the directions and it increases our show rate in both locations. If you'd like to see examples of these videos go to our resources page at: http://www.YourPracticeAutomated.com/Resources

The goal is systems and to train your people to run the systems correctly so that your business can run effectively without the need for you to be present.

That's true freedom.

Evaluate What's Working

In order for the people to run the systems without you, you must make your expectations for performance clear.

Once you've done that, you must inspect what you expect. I set up systems for my clients to do this in two specific ways: mystery shopping and surveys.

We regularly use mystery shoppers to test the performance of our team members. How was the client greeted? What was the state of the office? Did they smile? Did they use the script we created for setting an appointment on the phone?

We use mystery shoppers because we can look for very specific behaviors we've asked our staff to perform. The "client" will then come in with a checklist of specific things to look for. That checklist enables us to provide feedback to our staff in each area of the overall client experience.

Just like anything else in the business, you can systematize your mystery shopping to occur at specific intervals so that you are checking performance and giving feedback regularly.

The second tool we use is a customer satisfaction survey. I have the firms I consult ask their clients to rate their experience with the firm at various points in the sales process.

This allows us to do several things. First, we can give feedback to individual team members about their performance. Secondly, it allows us to look in greater detail at the client experience, compare it to other clients or prospects that have fallen out of the sale process and decided not to hire us, and then determine *what happened* throughout their experience that led them to change their minds. There is great power in having clients evaluate your firm.

Why implement mystery shopping *and* client surveys? Because the mystery shoppers are inspecting the steps you've outlined as part your sales process and focus on the implementation of these steps without being emotionally involved in the experience—they don't really need to get a divorce or file for bankruptcy—they don't react in the same way a client may react to the response by the receptionist or to the temperature in the room.

Clients often react strongly when something about the staff, the office, or the experience doesn't meet their expectations. And this reaction can make the difference between whether they hire or chose not to hire the firm for their case.

There's a saying and it goes like this: "In your business, as the business owner, there's what you want to be happening, what you think is happening and what is actually happening"

You must inspect what you expect in order to make sure the client experience you've outlined is being achieved.

Keep Kicking the Ball

As you're building your practice you've got to "keep the ball rolling" as they say. But *your* time is too valuable to spend your day kicking the ball over and over again. You must train other people to start kicking the ball for you.

When you've got the right people, in the right jobs, with the right attitudes and who are cross-trained in other areas within your practice you now have built a team that can start taking that ball down the field and scoring goals for you again and again.

It all starts with setting up the right management system to get the ball rolling in the right direction and keep it moving....whether you decide to come into the office or not.

Scott David Stewart on Management

One of the biggest things Rich really taught me was to look at management as a system. Growing up I always looked at building your product as a system—for us that's cases—but I'd never really looked at managing people as a system. Rich really opened my eyes up to putting together a process to help manage the people in the firm.

One of the first things we did was look at each position in the firm and analyze how that particular person operated within the firm, how they made the firm money, how they did their job, and to make sure that they focused only on activities that were high payoff activities for them.

Another thing Rich helped me do was to put a system in place for finding high quality people. As a law firm owner, you want to make sure that everyone running your business is a superstar.

Rich helped me put together classifications and job descriptions to identify what the job was, so we could then find the right person to fit that job. I now have a system in place, top down, to take a look at each individual person, what their job is, and how they are doing it.

But the most important thing is that we have a way to inspect what each individual person has done because we've developed reports. We know if the person is performing. We know if the system is performing. And we know if the law firm is performing.

Secret #3
Systematize Your Work Flow

Once you have the right people in the right jobs, you want to develop a system to manage their work flow. This is important because this is the system that ensures you are keeping the promises you have made to your clients.

I like to say that systems run your business and people run your systems. You can't have an Autonomous Business without both.

In addition to keeping your promises to your clients, a work flow management system also minimizes complaints against you to the bar association.

My clients who have implemented a work flow system have no concerns whatsoever about being reported to the Bar Association. They don't worry because they *know* that the work flow management system we've implemented virtually guarantees that they've done everything they agreed to do when they engage a client.

While it may be unnerving to have the bar peeking under the hood and looking at how you run your business, it's much less stressful when you know you have a system in place to ensure you get things done.

What is Work Flow Management?

I've already said that systematizing your work flow ensures that you keep your promises to your clients. The system that ensures this includes a detailed set of policies and procedures that have been thoroughly documented AND a system for measuring their adherence by your staff.

In order to manage your firm's work flow, you'll start by answering questions like these:

- How do things get done around here?
- How do we inspect what gets done around here?
- How do I measure what's working?
- How do I evaluate what's not working?
- Who does what and how do they do it?
- How can I consistently duplicate a high level of service?
- If I opened another location, do I have documented processes I could hand over to someone as the operations manual for the location?

That last question is the real kicker. If you want to find out how good or bad your systems are, try opening a new location!

Building a work flow management system starts with looking at what each person does—each task or process—and thoroughly documenting what they do.

Next, you need to compare what they are doing against what you want them to be doing. This is essential in order to meet the personal expectations you have set for your business.

Once you know what each person is supposed to do, you can then begin to track whether or not they are doing it. Only then can you be assured that the type of service you want to be delivered to your clients is being accomplished.

The "Secret Sauce" Example

When you analyze work flow you're trying to capture the recipe for how a person fulfills a particular part of their job description. Since it's very much like a recipe, I want to share the following example.

My grandmother made the most amazing pasta sauce in the world. She made an East Coast Italian, unbelievably amazing sauce. But nobody in our family knew how to make it. And the reason why nobody knew how to make this pasta sauce is because it wasn't passed down from generation to generation; it was just something my grandmother had learned from her mother.

The recipe wasn't written down. It was all in grandmother's head. People would ask her to write it down, but she couldn't!

She'd say, "It's all in my head! It's all in my head!" And it's likely she didn't know exactly what she was doing...she just did it.

Finally I said to my wife, "You have to go and watch her. And when you do I'll go with you and we will write it down. So when she begins to cut garlic and add the seasonings we can measure the quantities of each. Then we will be able to duplicate her process.

I learned that day that the fastest way to make a little Italian lady from Scranton, Pennsylvania mad is to stop her in the middle of making Italian sauce. But let me tell you, the end result was I went from having a wife who apologized for burning the toast when we first got married to a wife who makes the most amazing sauce in the world. And it's because we now can duplicate that recipe.

You'll do the exact same thing with your employees.

Have them write down everything they do in a process. Every task or process they've listed that they do in the course of the day needs to be analyzed and documented. Just like my grandmother's recipe. You need the recipe for every aspect of every job description.

This type of analysis gives you control of your workflow. It also positions your firm for expansion. When you have documented the policies and procedures that make one office successful, you will be able to open another office and be assured to consistently deliver a quality experience to your clients.

That's the value of systems.

You Must Decide How to Run Your Business

You may be full of ideas about how you want your practice to be run but if you're like most attorneys, you probably have little success in systematizing these ideas in a way that gets consistent performance from your staff.

Once you decide how you want your practice to run ask yourself, "What processes are in place to be sure the system is duplicable?"

Automating your work flow is the foundation you must have in place in order to grow and expand your practice. It's also one of the golden keys to achieving the freedom you deserve.

Secret #4
Make Marketing Your Top Priority

When you hear the word "marketing," what do you think of? Your full color ad on the back of the Yellow Book? Your 30 second spot on the local TV channel? The Val-Pak flyer you sent out last month?

Most people hear the word "marketing" and instantly think of what is really advertising. So before we go too much further, let me clarify the difference.

Marketing is the overall structure, plan, philosophy, process and system you have in place for promoting your services to your market.

Advertising is the media you use to carry out your marketing plan. Advertising includes TV, radio, newspaper, direct mail, Internet, pay per click ads, directory listings, pay per lead programs—all of the above are forms of advertising.

Your marketing plan is your overall system for communicating with your market.

Advertising is how you implement that plan.

My personal belief is that Marketing is 50% math, 30% systems and only 20% new ideas!

Why Marketing Matters

It's been said that today's consumer is bombarded by 10,000 marketing messages per day. TV, radio, bus benches, bill boards...all these vie for their attention.

Your marketing must stand out from all these messages.

In addition to standing out, your messages must stand out in more places than one. It used to be that the average number of contacts or exposures to a message before a prospect was ready to buy was estimated to be three to five. But with all the competition that figure is now estimated to be ten to thirteen or higher, depending upon your market and offer.

Marketing matters because it is the lifeblood of your business. Marketing is the system that brings leads through your doors from a multiplicity of sources. And for that reason alone it is vital that you have a marketing plan *and* a system for tracking which sources of leads are the most profitable.

Developing Your Unique Competitive Advantage (UCA)

The most important step you can take in your marketing is to develop your Unique Competitive Advantage statement or UCA.

Your unique competitive advantage answers the question, "Why should consumers decide to choose you over your competition?" That's it. And the easiest answer to that is, "Because it's *my firm*."

You are (or should be) the star of your firm. If you work with our team, we'll ensure that's the case.

"D" Pew is one of the only attorneys in Phoenix with both a tax and bankruptcy focus. His credentials became the source for Pew Law Center's UCA.

When we developed the UCA for Pew Law Center, we determined that it's the premier bankruptcy and tax relief law firm in Arizona.

The unique competitive advantage we have is that Pew Law Center can meet all your tax and bankruptcy needs without having to send you anywhere else. It's a one-stop-shopping proposal.

For example, when someone asks "D", "What do you do?" he has a clear answer.

He says, "We are the premier bankruptcy and tax relief law firm in the Valley."

The goal of the UCA is to make it clear to your market why they should choose you and your firm over the competition. It's also a handy way for you to have an answer when somebody asks you what it is that you do.

Your Unique Competitive Advantage statement becomes the heart of your marketing message.

The next thing you need to understand is your market...also known as your "who".

Understanding Your "Who"

It is of utmost importance to understand *exactly* to whom you are marketing.

You currently may not know who your market is but if you've been in practice for more than five years, you have a history of clients to draw on for this information.

If you have been in business for any length of time, you can go to your database and look at who you served. For example, one of my divorce attorney clients, Scott David Stuart had the demographic information on all the clients he had done business with in the past and was using case management software so that we could start by measuring all the data highlighting specific areas of interest.

We found out that his client base was 60% male between the ages of 35 and 47 with an average income of $75,000. And his most profitable cases that not only made him the most money, but also seemed to make up the biggest percentage of his business, had children. They were also white Anglo-Saxon Protestants—not Catholics, not Mormons, not Jews, but Protestants.

That is Scott David Stewart's "who". He didn't necessarily set out to attract that specific market segment. But he was able to identify what the data had to say about who was being attracted to his law firm.

That's not to say you couldn't create a marketing plan to target a specific market. You could. But in his case, we used the data to validate what was already working and making his practice profitable.

The data we received enabled us to drill down his marketing, messaging, and various other things that were in place and we used this to develop who he was as a firm.

Message to Market Match

Once you understand your Unique Competitive Advantage (your message) and your "who" (your market), your next step is to craft a message specifically for them and to launch it in the most appropriate media to attract your ideal client.

Your marketing plan should include a variety of media in order to reach your target market in multiple places at once:

- Print
- Online
- Social media
- Yellow pages
- "Real" media (i.e., TV, radio, etc.)
- Direct mail
- And so many more

But even if your message and market are completely matched, you still have one thing missing...an offer that gets prospects to contact you.

The Secret Key of Marketing

The greatest secret that so few attorneys understand is something called a "lead generation magnet."

A lead generation magnet...known as a lead magnet for short...is something informational or educational you offer to your prospective clients either for FREE or for a minimal charge.

This is the NEW REASON prospective clients will be calling your office. They will be calling to request the lead magnet you are offering.

[handwritten margin note: Credit Score report]

It may be in the form of:

- A real, genuine, in print book (i.e., *7 Tax Secrets the IRS Doesn't Want You to know* or *Is He Cheating? What You Need to Know About Divorce Before It's Too Late*)

- An audio CD you've recorded

- An e-book they can download from your website

- A checklist they can follow if attempting a DIY legal procedure

- A live event that educates them about their situation [Seminar]

The days of "Call Our Office" are over. The key to your success in marketing is to offer a lead magnet and then follow up religiously and relentlessly until they hire your firm.

Once you've established your Unique Competitive Advantage, you know your "who" and you've developed a free offer of information, you will be well on your way to achieving the freedom a wealthy attorney enjoys.

However, marketing is only part of the package. You must accompany your marketing program with a consistent tracking system that tells you which sources of leads are generating the most cash flow. You can then use those systems to guide your decision making about where to spend your marketing dollars.

That's the secret to turn marketing dollars from something you consider an "expense" to what is truly an "investment".

I'll cover this in more detail in the next chapter, "Consistently Generate New Leads."

Scott David Stewart on Marketing

Rich and I view marketing in much the same way. The marketing system is an overarching umbrella that covers a lot of different things including lead conversion and lead generation. But when you look at the marketing umbrella as a whole, you're including things such as:

- *What's our Internet marketing or web marketing strategy going to be?*
- *What is our offline strategy going to be?*
- *Does that include things such as radio, television, billboard, Yellow Book, Yellow Pages?*
- *Does it include something different like direct mail?*

What we did was to come back and ask, "What happens from the point the client calls the office?"

We started looking at the client experience. We looked at what we can do to change the client experience internally. This is still, in my opinion, part of the marketing strategy because the minute the client calls, comes in your office, and sits in your conference room, you're constantly doing things to let them know you're the person to hire.

We were able to put an entire system in place to cover every aspect of every experience concerning marketing.

Secret #5
Consistently Generate New Leads

Did you know that just understanding the difference between marketing and advertising (as we covered in the previous chapter) gives you a HUGE advantage over your competition?

You're now in a position to make more from your advertising dollars.

But there's one more *very* important secret you need to know...

Branding is Bunk!

Too many attorneys spend hundreds of THOUSANDS of dollars every year on branding. They think that the secret to wealth is plastering your face on every billboard, bus bench, shopping cart and TV screen in town.

They've been deceived into believing that brand awareness equates to dollars.

But that's simply not true.

The goal of your advertising is to generate leads. But here's how too many attorneys try to achieve this...

TV Commercial: "...just call our office!"

Radio Ad: "...just call our office!"

Yellow Book Ad: "...just call our office!"

If you're lucky, people will eventually call your office, but if you want to become a truly Autonomous Attorney, you'll need to be more sophisticated than that with your lead generation.

Capturing Leads

You can no longer leave the decision to the prospect as to whether or not they will call your office. These days savvy attorneys give prospects a compelling reason to call.

You MUST present an irresistible offer your prospects can't refuse!

I mentioned in the previous chapter that YOU should be your Unique Competitive Advantage. You should become the rock star of your business.

One of the ways I help clients achieve rock star status is by turning them into published authors.

Scott David Stewart uses a product called *E-Divorce Course*. He offers this course via an e-mail delivery system. But the only way to get on the list is by entering your contact information into a web form or by calling his office to request the book. His staff collects all their contact information, enabling the firm to follow up by phone, email and direct mail forever after. At our last count this course was generating a 4000% R.O.I.!

"D" Pew is the author of *Bankruptcy Secrets "They" Don't Want You to Know*. We offered this book during an early morning TV interview and generated 80 new leads. People called in to get the book...not to make an appointment. So we captured 80 new leads that have bankruptcy on their minds. All we have to do is keep following up with them until they are ready to have us solve their problems.

Branding is dead. Being an expert, celebrity, author is alive and well.

Every ad you place in every media source should be placed with the objective of generating leads and capturing contact information from prospects.

Multiplying and Tracking Your Sources of Leads

At Pew Law Center we have 175 lead sources. From TV to print ads, from direct mail to pay per click, we've got it all.

If we find a source that matches our "who," we place an ad and test it. We start small, test the source, and if it produces a decent ROI, we invest more.

How can we afford this much advertising?

We have a system in place to measure the results. Then we only invest in the sources that produce an acceptable Return on Investment.

How do we track all of these lead sources?

I was hoping you'd ask!

Pew Law Center has 175 unique phone numbers. Each phone number is assigned to a lead source. Our website has one number. Television Ad #1 has its own number. Each print ad will be assigned its own unique number.

Anytime a prospect responds to an ad by calling the phone number that person can be tracked directly to the source of the call. And because we use a whisper service on our line, we're able to input that information directly into our marketing automation system.

A whisper service means that when our staff answers the phone, just before the caller comes on the line they hear, "This call is from Lead Source #X." Then when they answer the call and take down the caller's contact information they also include the lead source that generated the call.

Because marketing is one of your biggest expenses, you absolutely MUST learn to manage this expense profitably if you want to become a wealthy attorney.

If you want more information about call tracking go here: www.YourPracticeAutomated.com/Resources

All These Lead Sources and All This Tracking Sounds Complicated

A few key benefits make tracking your lead generation efforts irresistible.

As I've already demonstrated, tracking your lead generation from source through to sale enables you to make better decisions about what to do with your money.

Tracking allows you to compare one lead source against another and consciously choose the best investment.

When you discover your average ROI from each lead source, you can almost make money at will by choosing to advertise there.

You can even predict the number of leads you should generate, how many typically turn into hires, and how much you will generate in total sales.

It's like you've built your very own cash machine.

If managing multiple lead sources and tracking each sounds complicated to you, it's really worth the time when you examine the payoff in the end.

If you like what you've heard so far but are starting to doubt your own abilities to manage a system like this, take heart. I've developed a turnkey system that puts your marketing and lead source tracking on autopilot.

To learn more about our automated practice building system, visit us online at www.YourPracticeAutomated.com

Secret #6
Convert New Leads
into Cash

In religion, a person "converts" when they change their mind and decide to walk a different path in life. Your goal in business is to "convert" a prospect...to influence them to change their minds and decide to do business with you...thus taking their life and their money down a new path.

However, conversion is a process. Rarely does anyone make the decision to "convert" or do business with you based on their first encounter. Your job is to move them from their first exposure to your business, step-by-step through the conversion *process* until they've decided to engage your services.

In a law practice, the stages in that process may look something like the pyramid below:

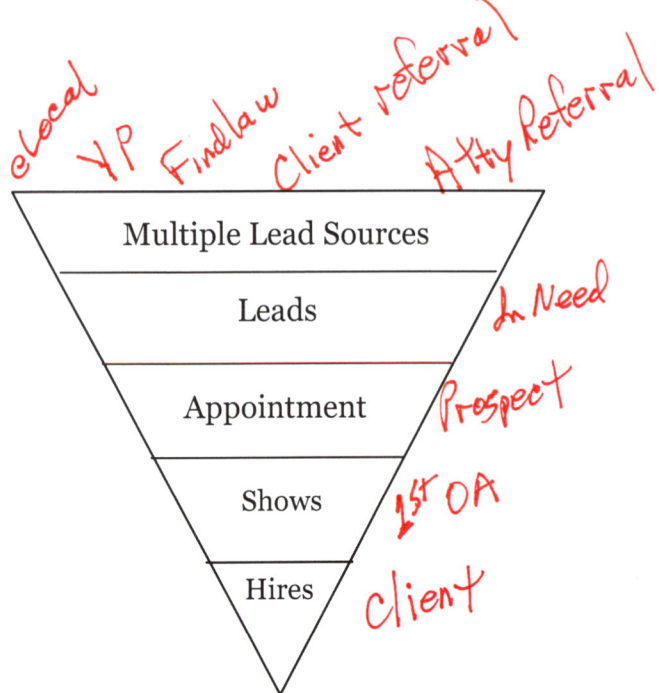

The first step in the conversion process is the prospect's exposure to your advertising which occurs at the lead source (i.e., website, newspaper, TV, Radio, Yellow Book, etc.).

The initial response occurs when the prospect becomes a new lead. For example, they might fill out a form on your website, complete a chat box or call into the office to request information. As soon as you have captured a piece of their contact information, the initial response was made and you have acquired a new lead.

Your next task is to set an appointment for the new lead to come into your office. As you well know, this is not an easy task. It is a decision influenced by many factors:

- Is the receptionist happy and welcoming?

- What is said when answering the phone?

- What is said when making outbound calls?

- What will you offer if they do come in?

- What does your website say about the initial consultation?

- How prepared is the prospect to take the next step?

- What do they hope to gain by making an appointment?

It is your responsibility to establish a system to manage the factors that influence the conversion process and to do everything to ensure an appointment is made...and kept.

Once an appointment is made, what do you do to ensure it is kept? Do you call to remind them? Send email reminders? Give them homework to complete before the appointment? Send a special package to their home?

At each step along the way, your duty to convert the prospect is once again renewed.

And in the final stage, when the prospect comes in for the initial consultation, you must control the environment and process that leads them to hire you.

Track Your Results to Improve Your Results

Once you begin tracking your results you will begin to see where your conversion efforts are succeeding...and where they are not.

Your next goal is to figure out why.

In the chapter on Management, we talked about using mystery shoppers and customer service evaluations to determine how your staff's performance is affecting the sales process. I'll make that recommendation again here.

In addition to mystery shoppers coming in for an appointment (which I highly recommend) you can also have them test your online chat service or give feedback on the persuasiveness of your website.

Client surveys will help you determine what's not working when it comes to soft skills and atmosphere. Yes, you can ask, "Did our office smell nice?" or "Did the receptionist smile and say good morning?" These are things you want to know.

How you go about improving your results is critical. You cannot simply say to your staff, "Hey, clients didn't think you were friendly enough. Will you please be friendlier when clients come in?"

In order to improve the client experience you have to outline behaviors that are measurable...behaviors that can be observed.

For example, rather than tell someone to be more friendly, you might say, "When someone walks in, I want you to make eye contact with each person in the party. I want you to say 'good morning' or whatever is appropriate for that time of day. Then I want you to offer them a seat, hand them a refreshment menu and take their order for a drink and a cookie. I want you to deliver the drink and cookie along with a napkin and a coaster, smile and make eye contact again, and say, 'Mr. Pew will be ready to receive you momentarily. If I can assist you in any way, please don't hesitate to ask.'"

Do you see how those instructions function like a checklist? Anyone in the room could watch that receptionist with a checklist in hand and check off whether or not she exhibited each behavior. That observation could easily be turned into a scored evaluation with a numeric evaluation that could be compared month over month and year over year.

I can't repeat enough...you must inspect what you expect. That's the secret to becoming an Autonomous Attorney.

Secret #7
Measure Your Success with Key Performance Indicators

If you tried to keep track of all the metrics I've outlined in this book on a weekly basis you'd probably end up overwhelmed.

When people are overwhelmed they tend to throw the baby out with the bath water.

There's no point in creating a measurement system that's destined to fail.

That's why I want you to focus on a set of Key Performance Indicators or KPIs.

KPIs give you a discrete set of metrics that let you take the pulse of your business easily and almost instantaneously.

Here are the KPIs I have all my clients focus on:

    Number of phone calls in and out
    Average time on phone
    Number of leads
    Lead source
    Cost per lead per lead source
    Number of appointments set as compared to

leads
Number of shows compared to appointments
Number of hires compared to shows
Cost per sale per lead source

As you can see, the KPI report is where many of the key metrics we've talked about all come together.

The great mystery is how to build a system that allows you to generate this information quickly and easily.

Systematizing Your KPI Report

In order to track financial metrics like Cost per Lead per Lead Source and Cost per Sale per Lead Source we set up a good-quality system in QuickBooks. Running all our transactions through QuickBooks makes a certain amount of the reporting a done deal. We put the information in so we can get the information out in the form of a KPI report.

In addition to QuickBooks, we use Infusionsoft software to set up reports that can identify all of the major reporting data necessary to measure number of leads, lead sources, number of appointments, number of shows, etc.

To find out more about Infusionsoft and how it can help your business go here:
www.YourPracticeAutomated.com/Resources

As a result, we can generate reports that show all leads and appointments set, the show rate, the hire rate, and who hired later. We can see how many cases were filed, how many Chapter 13's were confirmed, how many plans were filed, how many cases were dismissed, how many cases we converted.

Between QuickBooks and Infusionsoft, we can generate a KPI report (along with many others) at the touch of a button.

But what do we do with the reports? What is the objective?

Evaluating Your Progress

While the KPIs are valuable as a snapshot in time they become even more valuable when you conduct year-over-year, month-over-month or week-over-week comparisons.

The objective of tracking your KPIs is to detect trends in performance.

When I look at the KPIs for Pew Law Center, I can easily see if we are trending up or down, if one week's performance was worse than the week after.

We do everything by weeks so I can keep my finger on the pulse of the business.

We look at the KPIs and ask, "Are we up or are we down?" In retail it is called "comps". We take the time period versus the same time period from the previous year and review it. We look at the numbers and ask, "Are we going in the right direction or in the wrong direction? And is there something that is dramatically off that needs my attention right away?"

When the numbers are trending up, I am looking at it to figure out what we did right this week so that we can continue to repeat the behavior. When the numbers are down, I want to figure out what we can do better.

You use the numbers in the reports to point you toward the behaviors people are doing that are either making you money or losing you money. This is why I say that Marketing is 50% math and 30% systems.

Then you use your management and work flow systems to improve the problem points.

This is the type of simplicity that puts you on the path to becoming a wealthy attorney.

Scott David Stewart on KPIs

KPI's are the single most important system that you will ultimately develop. They tell you what systems are working, how they're working and what systems need to be fixed or inspected.

Your reports are going to be one click away. Your data is going to be right there in front of you whenever you need it.

Before I started working with Rich, I managed by my gut. When I first sat down with Rich, he would ask me for the numbers. I would say, "Well I think that it's X" or "I know that it's Y." But when he forced me to actually go and get the information and retrieve the data, it was virtually impossible. It sometimes took weeks to get the information and when I looked at it, I was wrong.

Now all the info is one click away. My firm administrator gives me a report every month. It shows how many leads were generated, how many consults were set, what the set rate was, what the show rate was, and what the conversion rate was at the consultation. We know what each attorney's consultation % is, what their average client hire rate is.

All those things were impossible for me to retrieve before working with Rich.

Probably one of the biggest things that has happened since we started working together is that I went from being an attorney to managing the attorneys.

I no longer have a case load. I meet regularly with the attorneys to review their case load, but I operate the business now. I run the law firm.

Prior to working with Rich I was just another cog in what was going on. My life has changed dramatically since that point and I owe it all to Rich.

Bonus Secret
Automate Your Systems

I say that we're keeping it simple. I imagine you're probably wondering how any of this could be called simple at all!

We're measuring how leads progress through the sales process. We're sending out appointment reminders, no show reminders, satisfaction questionnaires, making phone calls, tracking phone calls. How can this be simple?

The secret behind the simplicity is automation.

D Pew on Automating Your Practice

There's something about having someone else hold you accountable and putting the systems into place to hold everyone in the business accountable.

We have these systems in place now. So instead of having to go through the painful ordeal of setting it up and implementing it, it's there. Now it's just a matter of tweaking it here and there.

We have it set up to keep growing and growing. In one year we grew over 500%. It's a beautiful thing to actually sit back and look at what we've done and just watch it grow. It's exciting. We continue to meet new goals and hit new levels every month.

A Final Word from the Author

I truly hope you enjoyed reading this short book on the *DNA of The Autonomous Attorney* as much as I enjoyed writing it.

My primary aim in life is work with as many likeminded entrepreneurs who truly want to be helped and who will actually take action and implement the ideas we lay out for them.

If you're one of those attorneys who considers themselves an entrepreneur first and an attorney second and you'd like to learn from someone who's been there, in the trenches and has real life experience getting results for small and solo law firms, contact me. I'd be happy to offer you a free 15 minute strategy session. Just send an email to Richard@YourPracticeAutomated.com or call 602-429-9955.

My hope today is that I brought value to our time together.

Building a better business, one system at a time...

Warmest Regards,

Richard James

Made in the USA
Charleston, SC
28 August 2013